W9-BXT-853

DRAKE

★ FAMOUS MUSIC STAR ★

Big Buddy Books

An Imprint of Abdo Publishing
abdopublishing.com

BIG
BUDDY **POP** BIOGRAPHIES

KATIE LAJINESS

LONDON PUBLIC LIBRARY

abdopublishing.com

Published by Abdo Publishing, a division of ABDO, PO Box 398166, Minneapolis, Minnesota 55439.
Copyright © 2018 by Abdo Consulting Group, Inc. International copyrights reserved in all countries.
No part of this book may be reproduced in any form without written permission from the publisher.
Big Buddy Books™ is a trademark and logo of Abdo Publishing.

Printed in the United States of America, North Mankato, Minnesota.
052017
092017

THIS BOOK CONTAINS
RECYCLED MATERIALS

Cover Photo: Jordan Strauss/Invision/AP.
Interior Photos: Aby Baker / Contributor/Getty (p. 27); Andreas Arnold/picture-alliance/dpa/AP
    Images (p. 17); ASSOCIATED PRESS (pp. 5, 11, 19, 25); Christopher Polk/AMA2016/Contributor/
    Getty (p. 23); Everett Collection Inc./Alamy Stock Photo (p. 15); galit seligmann/Alamy Stock
    Photo (p. 9); John Shearer/Staff/Getty (p. 13); n8n photo/Alamy Stock Photo (p. 21); REUTERS/
    Alamy Stock Photo (p. 9); The Photo Access/Alamy Stock Photo (p. 29); ZUMA Press, Inc./Alamy
    Stock Photo (p. 6).

Coordinating Series Editor: Tamara L. Britton
Graphic Design: Jenny Christensen

Publisher's Cataloging-in-Publication Data

Names: Lajiness, Katie, author.
Title: Drake / by Katie Lajiness.
Description: Minneapolis, MN : Abdo Publishing, 2018. | Series: Big buddy
    pop biographies | Includes bibliographical references and index.
Identifiers: LCCN 2016962360 | ISBN 9781532110603 (lib. bdg.) |
    ISBN 9781680788457 (ebook)
Subjects: LCSH: Drake, 1986- --Juvenile literature. | Actor--Canada --Biography-
    -Juvenile literature. | Rap musicians--Canada--Biography--Juvenile literature.
    | Singers--Canada--Biography--Juvenile literature.
 Classification: DDC 782.421649092 [B]--dc23
LC record available at http://lccn.loc.gov/2016962360

CONTENTS

MUSIC SENSATION 4

SNAPSHOT 5

FAMILY TIES 6

EARLY YEARS..................................... 8

RISING STAR 10

BUILDING A CAREER 14

MIXING SOUNDS................................18

BUSINESSMAN...................................20

AWARD SHOWS 22

GIVING BACK 24

SCREEN TIME................................... 26

BUZZ...28

GLOSSARY 30

WEBSITES..31

INDEX 32

MUSIC SENSATION

Drake is an **award**-winning **hip-hop** artist, **rapper**, and songwriter. Since 2006, he has **released** many hit songs that top the music charts. Millions of people watch Drake's music videos. Fans chat about him on **social media**.

SNAPSHOT

NAME:
Aubrey Drake Graham

BIRTHDAY:
October 24, 1986

BIRTHPLACE:
Toronto, Ontario, Canada

POPULAR ALBUMS:
*Thank Me Later, Take Care,
Nothing Was the Same, Views*

FAMILY TIES

Aubrey Drake Graham was born on October 24, 1986, in Toronto, Ontario, Canada. His parents are Dennis and Sandi Graham. They separated when Aubrey was five years old. He does not have any brothers or sisters.

Drake's mother worked as an English teacher in Canada.

WHERE IN THE WORLD?

CANADA

QUEBEC

ONTARIO

Vermont

Toronto

Michigan

New York

UNITED STATES

Ohio

Pennsylvania

ATLANTIC
OCEAN

N
W E
S

EARLY YEARS

As a child, Aubrey lived with his mom in Toronto. There, he attended a **Jewish** school. At 13, Aubrey had a **bar mitzvah**.

Outside of school, Aubrey played hockey and acted in the Young People's Theater.

Aubrey's dad plays music in Memphis, Tennessee. So, Aubrey often traveled 15 hours to see his dad. There, Aubrey learned a lot about music.

Memphis is known for its live music.

Drake's dad appeared in the video for "Worst Behavior" from Drake's *Nothing Was the Same* album.

RISING STAR

When Aubrey was 14, he was a TV actor. For seven seasons, he was on *Degrassi: The Next Generation*. During that time, he also wrote and recorded his **rap** songs.

In 2006, Aubrey **released** a **mixtape** called *Room for Improvement*. The next year, he put out another mixtape, *Comeback Season*. It included "Replacement Girl," which became a major hit.

In 2007, Aubrey (*second from right*) and his *Degrassi* castmates appeared on MTV to promote the show in New York City, New York.

Aubrey wanted to spend more time making music. In 2008, he left the show and changed his name to Drake.

The next year, **rapper** Lil Wayne heard Drake's *Comeback Season*. Lil Wayne thought Drake was very talented. So, he invited Drake to join his music tour.

Drake and rapper Lil Wayne (*right*) performed together at the 2009 BET Awards.

BUILDING A CAREER

In 2009, a New York radio station played Drake's "Best I Ever Had" more than 1,300 times. This helped him get a recording contract. Then he put out his third **mixtape**, *So Far Gone*.

Drake's first album, *Thank Me Later*, came out in 2010. A year later, he **released** *Take Care*. People bought more than 4 million copies!

In 2010, Drake greeted his fans before the BET Awards in Los Angeles, California.

Drake was on his way to becoming one of the most popular **hip-hop** artists and **rappers** in the country. In 2012, he **released** *Nothing Was the Same*. The album sold more than 1 million copies in just six weeks.

In 2016, *Views* came out. In six days, more than 1.2 million people bought it. This album reached number one on the Billboard 200 chart.

DID YOU KNOW?

As of 2016, Drake has the most number-one hits for a solo artist on Billboard's Hot 100 chart.

Drake traveled to Germany to give a concert in 2014.

MIXING SOUNDS

Drake often works with other singers and **rappers**. He has **performed** with Eminem, Jay Z, and Rihanna.

In 2016, Drake sang "Work" with Rihanna. Their song stayed on the Billboard Hot 100 chart for 36 weeks. He also sang "One Dance" with WizKid and Kyla. This song reached number one on the Billboard music chart.

Drake presented Rihanna with the 2016 MTV Video Vanguard Award.

BUSINESSMAN

In addition to his music, Drake owns many companies under the name October's Very Own (OVO). In 2011, he started a clothing line. Within five years, he had stores in Toronto, Los Angeles, California, and New York City, New York.

Each year, Drake also puts on OVO Fest in Toronto. Big names such as Eminem, Jay Z, Kanye West, and Lil Wayne have **performed** at this festival.

Drake performed at the 2012 OVO Fest at the Molson Canadian Amphitheater.

AWARD SHOWS

Drake has won many **awards** for his music. In 2010, Drake **performed** at the **Grammy Awards** before he even **released** an album.

In 2012, Drake won a Grammy for Best **Rap** Album for *Take Care*. Five years later, he took home two more Grammy Awards.

DID YOU KNOW?

In 2016, Drake set a record for 13 American Music Award nominations.

Drake accepted the Favorite Rap/Hip-Hop Album award at the 2016 American Music Awards.

GIVING BACK

Drake is known for giving back. Drake plays in **celebrity** basketball and softball games to help others.

Music is another way Drake helps people. He gifted a recording studio to Strawberry Mansion High School in Philadelphia, Pennsylvania.

Drake's money helped students at Strawberry Mansion High School learn about music production.

In 2013, Drake traveled home to Canada to help with a Toronto basketball event.

SCREEN TIME

Drake still enjoys acting. He has been on *Saturday Night Live* twice. There, Drake acted in funny **skits**. And, he **performed** his music.

DID YOU KNOW ?
Drake was a voice actor in the animated movie *Ice Age: Continental Drift*.

Drake (*right*) had a role in *Anchorman 2: The Legend Continues*. He played a character called Soul Brother.

BUZZ

DID YOU KNOW?

In 2017, Drake won a Grammy Award for Best Rap Song for "Hotline Bling."

Drake had a very successful 2016! His music was the most popular on Spotify, an online music-streaming service.

His music keeps getting bigger and better. In 2017, Drake **released** his next album, *More Life*. As his fame continues, Drake's fans are eager to see what he does next!

Drake's Summer Sixteen tour is the highest-grossing hip-hop tour of all time.

GLOSSARY

award something that is given in recognition of good work or a good act.

bar mitzvah a ceremony and celebration of a Jewish boy who turns 13 and attains the religious duties and responsibilities of an adult.

celebrity a famous or celebrated person.

Grammy Award any of the awards given each year by the National Academy of Recording Arts and Sciences. Grammy Awards honor the year's best accomplishments in music.

hip-hop a form of popular music that features rhyme, spoken words, and electronic sounds. It is similar to rap music.

Jewish of or related to Judaism, which is a religion based on laws recorded in the Torah.

mixtape a compilation of songs recorded (as onto a cassette tape or a CD) from various sources.

perform to do something in front of an audience.

rap a type of music in which the words of a song are spoken to a beat. A rapper is someone who raps.

release to make available to the public.

skit a brief sketch in play form.

social media a form of communication on the Internet where people can share information, messages, and videos. It may include blogs and online groups.

WEBSITES

To learn more about Pop Biographies, visit **abdobooklinks.com**. These links are routinely monitored and updated to provide the most current information available.

INDEX

Anchorman 2: The Legend Continues (movie) **27**

awards **4, 13, 15, 19, 22, 23, 28**

California **15, 20**

Canada **5, 6, 8, 20, 25**

charity work **24, 25**

Comeback Season (mixtape) **10, 12**

Degrassi: The Next Generation (television show) **10, 11, 12**

Eminem **18, 20**

family **6, 8, 9**

Germany **17**

Ice Age: Continental Drift (movie) **26**

Jay Z **18, 20**

Kyla **18**

Lil Wayne **12, 13, 20**

More Life (album) **28**

MTV **11, 19**

music charts **4, 16, 18**

New York **11, 14, 20**

Nothing Was the Same (album) **5, 9, 16**

October's Very Own **20, 21**

Pennsylvania **24, 25**

religion **8**

Rihanna **18, 19**

Room for Improvement (mixtape) **10**

Saturday Night Live (television show) **26**

So Far Gone (mixtape) **14**

social media **4**

Spotify **28**

Strawberry Mansion High School **24, 25**

Take Care (album) **5, 14, 22**

Tennessee **8, 9**

Thank Me Later (album) **5, 14**

Views (album) **5, 16**

West, Kanye **20**

Wizkid **18**

Young People's Theater **8**